I HAD CANCER,
CANCER
NEVER
HAD ME

AUTHORED BY
CHANTELL WINDHAM
WRITTEN BY
LESA BUTLER

For information, please contact :
W : **www.shepublishingllc.com**
E : **info@shepublishingllc.com**

Book Cover and Title Page design by Michelle Phillips of
CHELLD3 3D VISUALIZATION AND DESIGN

ISBN: 978-1-953163-45-5

First Edition: July 2022

10 9 8 7 6 5 4 3 2 1

CONTENTS

DEDICATION

This book is dedicated to my mother, Juanita Duplanter. Mom, Thank you for all your love, support, and sacrifice from my birth through your departure. There are no words sufficient to express the monumental impact you continue to have upon my life. Though you are absent in body, your spirit and wisdom remain forever etched in my soul. Thank you, Mom. I will honor you and be a testament of God's love and faith.

ACKNOWLEDGE MENTS

- ✗ My husband, Earl: For coming through with all my outrageous requests without complaining. Every slice of Giordano's and sip of iced coffee made my day!
- ✗ My Iowa Family: Chrissy, Mantez, Kenna, Nisha, Aunt Dee, Uncle Jr., Paula, Khyler, Makaiyo, Neka, Ty, and Tisha-Your visits throughout my cancer process meant more to me than you could ever know!
- ✗ Cousins: My first, second, and third cousins from all over the country for your tokens of love!
- ✗ My Sister-Friends: My best friend Collette, and sistahs Carla, Jamie, Kendra, and Lynda. Ladies, thank you for loaning me your strength and belief when mine refused to kick in.

- **My In-Laws and Extended Family:** The dinners, visits, and prayers were invaluable!
- **Sheila:** The countless hours you spent talking me off the ledge, smuggling snacks, and encouraging me to laugh instead of cry made all the difference!
- **My Angel:** Thank you for spending time with Mom and Aunt Dee when I was too tired to entertain. Oh, and, thanks for the popsicles too!
- **Burnham School:** For being an amazing extended family!
- **Chicago Bears:** I will always remember the way you made me feel like a quarterback burning up the turf to score the winning touchdown!
- **Sam Acho:** You took time out of your busy schedule to come to my school and fulfill my life-long dream of meeting a Bears team member and attending a game. That was everything!
- **The Oncology Staff at the University of Chicago:** For providing honest, timely feedback and treatment. Shout out to my nurses for giving me the space to be unapologetically me, while I sang, danced, and laughed my cares away!
- **Betty:** Thank you for always adjusting your schedule to sit with me during chemo, and

for being my voice when I was too tired or sick to complain.

- My Girl, Lesa: Thank you for painting this picture with our words and reminding me that my story deserves to be heard!
- My Publisher, Shenitha: Thank you for putting the finishing touches on my dream!
- Last, but certainly not least, my children: Elijah and Rachel: Giving up was not an option because you were my reason to keep pushing. I love you!

MY BREAST FRIENDS

(Fellow Cancer Champions)

Aunt Lou

Ms. Colton

Aunt Trena

Cousin Deenie

Cousin Tangla

Karla

Malissa

Ericka

Ms. Jeon

Ms. Dorsey

Ms. Linda

Ms. Robinzine

Ms. Julia

Ms. Velma

CANCER SUCKS

Hi, I'm Chantell. I was an ordinary woman, living an ordinary life, until an extraordinary obstacle jumped into my path. That uninvited party crasher was cancer. Oh, and I don't mean the Zodiac sign (shout out to all the Cancers out there). I mean the dreaded Big "C." It was Stage 2 breast cancer to be exact. Can you believe it? It came for me, and I didn't send for it. The nerve! Little did the Big "C" know that it had run up on another Big "C," otherwise known as The Chan.

Although I was caught totally by surprise and off guard, I was equipped for the rundown. Not because I was a great superhero already, but because my ordeal would turn me into one. Little did I know that one cold December day in 2017 the good Lord would call me in to be fitted for my cape. He was preparing me to defeat the dastardly villain that left me breastless in Chicago, and to beat cancer no matter how much it sucked. God was about to reveal how EXTRAORDINARY I am after all.

Oh, and by the way, the overused, cliché-ish slogan is right. **Cancer does suck!**

What It Means to Live

By Larry Brookins II

TO LIVE IS TO PERSEVERE
When it seems, the end is near
And to rise and fight
While conquering your fears
TO LIVE IS TO LOVE
Our fellow man and the Lord above
To pursue this with passion
Because love is a word of action
TO LIVE IS TO FORGIVE
When you're wronged, it hurts, that's true
But forgiveness isn't for them
You must do it for you
LIVING WILL BE TOUGH SOMETIMES
No, it is not always fun
But I count it all joy
I've learned to overcome
I THANK GOD IT HASN'T BEEN ALL EASY

Like when I was a kid Because of my trials I've learned what it truly means to live!!

"I want to live. I give God the glory and final say over my body and soul. I want to live and be a testimony of his power and strength."

-Chantell Windham

On the evening of December 17, 2017, my existence was forever altered. The nuclear bomb dropped on me that day left me temporarily broken, desperately struggling to put back together the pieces of the life I had worked so hard to build. I'm not talking about the bomb the R & B group The Gap Band was jamming about in the 80's. No, this bomb was more than about a wounded ego. This was the night I found out that I had breast cancer.

I believe there is a moment in everyone's life that tests one's spiritual, mental, and physical resolve. This was my moment. Never in a thousand millennia could I fathom what I had just heard. It just didn't make sense. How does a perfectly healthy person suddenly develop breast cancer? I mean, one second, I was sneaking off to the thrift stores scoring steals and deals, hiding my bags from my husband (Dangit, I just outed myself!) Then I blinked, and I was sitting in a chair with tubes hanging out of my chest. I just could not understand it, nor did I initially want to accept it.

I took strong exception to this predicament. Stage 2 breast cancer to be exact. This was one ball I wanted to kick back over to the other team! All I could think about was the effect my diagnosis would have on all associated with me. My children, my husband, my family, my LIFE. The thoughts raced through my head a thousand miles per nanosecond. I inwardly acknowledged the borderline narcissistic question that repeatedly entered my mind, "How would they survive without me?" I had always been the backbone, the go-to, the fixer, and the analytical person. I was the glue that held it all together.

No, no, this would never do. This would not, and could not, be my Waterloo. I had to fight. With every ounce of everything within me, I had to fight. Cancer picked the wrong one this time! There was far too much to live for, for me to submit and surrender. This would be my toughest battle to date, but I was ready. With the help of the Almighty God and love of family and friends, I was ready for all of it.

"Wait a minute, they were just nourishing him!
NOW THEY'RE KILLING YOU?"
-Rachel Windham

As the "old folks" say, "Out of the mouth of babes." This statement and subsequent question were my daughter's reaction to my breast cancer diagnosis. I stood there dazed and confused, struggling to figure the whole thing out. How does someone go from near-perfect health to missing eyebrows and eyelashes the next? I wanted to save money on eyebrow waxes, but this was ridiculous!

It felt as if that cold Wednesday evening in December of 2017 had started the Friday before. When the phone played its incoming call sonata, I was so busy it almost went unnoticed. I recognized the number on caller ID immediately. Reflecting on it now, I guess I should have been more worried. Considering why the person was calling, I suppose more concern would have been in order. For some reason, though, I just didn't feel it at that moment. Then the piano dropped on my head and snapped me into reality. Suddenly, the room began to spin.

"Chantell, it's cancer. We need to begin treatment right away." I'm quite sure more was said after that, but I didn't hear any of it. At that point Charlie Brown's teacher may as well have been talking. Darnit! Talk about an inconvenient truth! That was NOT the news I wanted to hear. Something along the lines of, "My dear, there's been a terrible mistake. Tests were all clear," would have been more palatable. Man, let me tell you, that news tasted like that Father John's cough syrup my grandmother used to give us when we had the slightest hint of the sniffles. It was bitter, nasty, and made my jaws quiver. Alas, the reality was that this was not a common cold, and it would take a heck of a lot more than Father John's to make it go away.

Who had time for a breast cancer diagnosis? Certainly not me, although I could hear the great motivational speaker Les Brown say, "Perhaps we could select a more convenient time. Next week, maybe? Next month?" Come to think of it, when would have been a better time to hear that you have Stage 2 breast cancer and could die? After the Superbowl would have been better, much better. At least I would have been full of snacks and full to the brim of adrenaline and dopamine!

That night sleep came over for a lengthy game of hide and seek. Yup, that night's slumber session was a wash. Breast cancer? What the whaaaaat? How was this going to affect my family, especially my mom? I just fought like hell to become a mother! Who was going to cook the chicken and biscuits? Who was going to tell my fourth graders for the umpteenth time that area and perimeter are not the same thing? I just knew I was being pranked. Those darn cameras had better not be recording me with my hair all over my head. This could not be happening.

But it was, and there was much to consider. The thought that kept running through my mind that night like Allyson Felix was, "How will this impact my family?" That's just who I am. I was raised to be more concerned about others than myself. I needed to make sure that somebody was going to be able to cook the chicken while I received my treatment. If you think I'm joking about frying chicken as an initial point of concern after receiving my diagnosis, you don't know my family. Ever seen a hungry toddler posted up in the kitchen staring down the stove with a plastic Elmo spoon in his hand? You get the picture.

How did this whole cancer thing unfold? Let me take you back...

A hard head makes a soft behind. Does that statement resonate with you? Well, I can tell you that if it didn't mean a thing to me before, it does now. I was on the straight and narrow road when I went in for my routine mammogram around 2015. The path became crooked when I neglected to return for a follow up visit when the doctor found abnormal cells in my breasts. Let me say that again, I did not return to find out why there were abnormal cells in my body. In fact, it was about 2 years later before I went back, but by then it was too late.

My reasons for lack of follow-up were important, right? I was busy. I was a wife, mother, educator, daughter, sister, and friend. Sports, lesson planning, and cooking chicken for my family took a front seat to my health. Though I loved my stepdaughter to pieces, and raised her as my own, my dream of having a biological child of my own was finally materializing. The road to motherhood was long and hard, but it was worth it. I had waited YEARS for this miracle. Finally, after multiple attempts, the Lord saw fit to put a bun in my oven. THIS was my focal point. I guess it didn't occur to me that raising my miracle baby would be difficult if I wasn't around to do it. Go figure that!

Thank goodness my primary care physician was on it! "Okay now, you've had the baby. What's the problem?" The tone of her voice convicted me sternly. It left me feeling like I used to when my mother asked me why I hadn't cleaned up my room yet. "Hmmmm, I contemplated, what *was* the problem?" My procrastination. That was the darn problem. I was fancy because motherhood was on the horizon. My doctor backed me 100% on that, but my health was also important to her. She was hearing no more excuses. "Get your butt in here!"

I got my butt in there and my life has not been the same since. My PCP (primary care physician) did some tests and wasn't pleased with what she saw because the next thing I knew I was in the radiologist's office. My doctor had mentioned "the big C," but it didn't get me riled up. It flew in one ear and out the other in a microsecond. Ha! Cancer? Me? No way! I finally got the baby I begged God for, and life was amazing! There's no way He would give this track runner a hurdle *that* high to jump over!

You know, it's mighty funny how quickly life will put you in your place and humble you. Crow, anyone? I had a crow wing dipped in mild sauce the day I shadowed the door of the radiologist's office. My daughter was with me and had no clue as to where we were or why we were there. I can remember staring at the pictures of women's breasts and various medical posters on the walls, hoping my daughter was oblivious to them. That was a conversation that, at that point, I didn't deem necessary to have. Little did I know how off that train of thought was.

Walking into the x-ray room was not a big deal to me that day. It was just routine, right? I was there as a formality, just so they could apologize for taking time out of my busy schedule and tell me it was a false alarm. When the radiologist took pictures of my breasts it wasn't a big deal, since that was the reason for my visit. Then, things took a turn when the tech began taking snaps of my underarms. I was sitting there thinking, "What in the world?" Even at *this* point, no alarms are going off. It is absolutely amazing the level of denial the human mind is capable of, just remarkable.

I was soaking up the African sun on that river called denial until the nurse came back in and gave me *the* hug. You know the one. The one that the mothers at the church give you right after you give an especially sad testimony. The kind where they rub the middle of your back in a circle like your mama does when you're congested. The type that makes you say, "Oh crap, something ain't right." It was not the hug I wanted right after cancer detection x-rays. That was never a good sign. "It's all right, baby. You're gonna be alright." That's what she said to me with that look in her eyes. My heart sunk. "I'm 99% sure it's breast cancer."

After the initial shock wore off that felt like people's description of a jellyfish sting, I gathered myself and dashed out into the waiting room. My daughter had been patiently sitting in the waiting room the entire time. The fact that the doctor was fired up with irritation at the person who mentioned cancer without concrete evidence to that effect meant nothing. Just the thought of that menace beginning with a "C" made me feel some type of way. All I could think was that I had to get her home without falling apart. Talk about a long drive home!

Then in December of 2017, on a Wednesday night, the worst was confirmed. It felt like all the wind was knocked out of me when I heard those words indicating I had cancer. You will see this date repeated throughout this book because it is forever etched in my mind. Just as December is associated with the bitter, freezing cold of winter, this December commenced a frozen period in my life.

I knew my children would want to know who was cooking. I would have to make sure I left clear instructions with my husband on the location of all medicines, toddler underwear, and hidden snacks. My Lord, then there was my mother. As sick as she was, the wild horses would have to be tamed to keep her from riding them to come to my aid from the next state over. Not to mention my Iowa family, including my siblings. They would try to get into a fist fight with the cancer cells themselves. Disclosing the news to these folks was going to be quite the situation. In the following pages I will let you in on how hearing the news went with those I care about the most.

SURVIVOR

IT WAS NEVER PROMISED THAT PAIN AND LOSS
would never come our way.
Only that we are Overcomers
and obstacles do not come to stay.
We are given the strength and power
hope to continue to stand
and allow the survivor within us
to grow and to expand.
THERE IS LIGHT IN THE DARKNESS
and comfort for the pain
There is fortitude to maintain
and grace to live again.
There is endurance to stand
and the will to not give in
Wisdom to know that no matter what
we are guaranteed a win.
THE JOY WE ONCE HAD
will come around once more
and on the mighty eagle's wings
we will rise and soar.
For we are survivors
made to overcome.
Filled with courage to fight
No matter what may come.

--Anonymous

Mom

"Okay, we're getting ready to fight."

My mom was sitting in her favorite chair at my house when I got the news. I remember that 6pm call in December of 2017 like it was yesterday. Mom slid into town a few days prior to that pivotal conversation to help me out with the grandbabies, as she did regularly since my stepfather died. She had been his caretaker, so she had extra time on her hands to bless us with her presence. I loved my mom. She was one special lady. Like so many people who pressed their way out of dysfunction, sometimes she won, sometimes she was on the ropes, but she never stepped outside of the ring. I don't judge my mom for her difficulties. She did the best she could with what she knew.

Now, don't get it twisted, my mom was much bigger than her struggles. She was a shining star who got hit upside the head with life's bricks, then picked them up and built a wall of resilience. Mom gave birth to me at the tender age of 16, but that didn't stop her. She graduated a full year early! My mama was smart and did not play around when it came to education.

Oh, and did I mention that she kept everybody's hair slayed and layed all the time? Yes, she did. Her hair, my hair, and my sister's hair were always fried, dyed, and laid to the side. She extended this gift to the women in the family, as well as others in the neighborhood. She loved hair so much that she went to cosmetology school. Not only did she graduate and receive her license, but she leveled up and became an instructor! Now I know where I got my teacher genes.

I must pause the party and brag on my mama for a few minutes. Her patience and calm, soothing voice made her a superstar in my book. These qualities were particularly useful in her work as a preschool teacher, which, in turn, proved to be indispensable in her interactions with my son. She was the world's greatest grandma, hands down (hopefully, I will be runner up someday). Mom always told us we could do and be anything we wanted, without limitation. "You want to be an astronaut? Cool. Let's find out when the next trip to the moon is so we can get a seat." "You want to train tigers to jump through fiery hoops? Great. The UniverSoul Circus is coming to town next week. See if we can have a sit down with the person over the animal tricks division."

I kid you not, this is exactly how conversations with my mother would go whenever we shared our dreams and aspirations. She was a teacher at heart, always looking for a touchpoint to connect us with our ambitions. She always knew just how much to push us.

Truthfully, I don't know if I would have had the discipline and where-with-all to earn three degrees without her constantly pushing me to excel. My mother couldn't help me a lot financially, but she more than made up for it in every other way.

When I ended the call with the doctor that fateful Wednesday night, my mom was right there, as usual. My mom was always right there. I knew I had to tell her, but it's not something I was itching to do. When I first opened my mouth to share the news, it was a re-enactment of the scene in the Disney classic The Little Mermaid when Ariel opened her mouth to sing but silence decided to jump out instead. Upon further contemplation, crooning the words could have made them more acceptable, even entertaining. I wonder what beat would have made "Mom, I have breast cancer" pop. One of Missy Elliot's iconic beats, or Pharrell's.

At any rate, her reaction was calm, but not at all shocking. "Alright, we're getting ready to fight," were her exact words. This response was not by any means a surprise. She was a fighter, a warrior. It was in her blood. She came from a long line of women who took life's lemons and made vats of lemonade. She was not easily rattled or broken by much. She took everything in stride. I guess that's where I get it from. It's interwoven into the fabric of my being.

Zena, Warrior Princess, came out when I told her what the doctor said that evening. I am fairly sure that if cancer were a person, the ultimate beatdown would have taken place that night! That woman did not play about her kinfolks! Oh yes, at this point, there is something I need to add to the story about my mom. When I received my diagnosis, she had been ill for some time. In fact, when she came into town to help me with the kids after my initial visit with the radiologist, I was concerned about the toll the visit would take on her. For years, my sister and I had taken her back and forth to the hospital for various heart conditions and other medical concerns. This contributed to my apprehension about telling her at first.

Although I prided myself on my ability to take life's crap with a smile, I was shook (*this is a term the young people used to mean highly disturbed*). When I hit the red "end" button on my phone, all I could do was drag my body to where my mom was sitting and put my head in her lap. True to form, she rubbed it in a circle like she used to when I was sick as a child and told me it was fighting time. Words can't express what that meant to me in that exact space in time. There is nothing like having your mom right in the ditch with you when life pushes you in.

Trying to sleep that Wednesday night was pointless. All I could think about was the effect it would have on my mother. Of course, I was worried about my husband and children also, but they weren't sick. My mom was. Although she had long-time struggles with illness, she was my mom. You only get one of those,

15

you know? She was always somewhere close whenever something went down. Even if all she could do was tell me everything was going to be alright, she made her presence felt. She was strong, but I didn't know how this one was going to play out. Would she be able to take the news? Would it be too much for her? Everybody has a breaking point, and I didn't want any camel's backs being broken by this piece of straw.

That first night was about me. That was my night to fall apart and allow her to comfort me. I gave myself time to sit in the shock of the diagnosis, with her reassurance that everything was going to be fine. The next morning, though, was all about my mom. I can recall moving ever so slowly down the stairs and catching a glimpse of her, suddenly remembering she was sick also. That moment sent me reeling back into reality. "Look, we gotta get it together. I've got to be here for her." That was the moment I grasped that this new "development" brought with it a higher level of relatability between my mother and I. Sure, we were both sick, but this was not the commonality I wanted to add to our repertoire. We now had to encourage each other through the roughest, toughest season. We were both fighting for our lives together.

Fight with and for me she did. She showed up and showed out during the storms of my cancer treatment. She was right there, holding a stadium-sized umbrella the entire time. To this day, I don't know what she was *really* thinking as she watched me endure countless chemo treatments, but she had "unbothered" written all over her face. Of course, she was bothered, but she never let it show. My mother's poker face could rival any back-alley card shark. She always carried with her the spirit of fearlessness and strength that I so desperately needed to make it through. I will always remember the champion my mother was throughout my process. She fought courageously for us both until she passed away on July 18, 2022.

The year prior to my cancer battle my mother put on the armor of God and fought her own skirmishes with respiratory ailments and stroke, which eventually took her from us. During that time, I was her armor bearer, standing dutifully at her side whenever I could. We sat together for hours watching reality TV, snacking mercilessly, and giggling like schoolgirls. Little did anyone know that almost one year later exactly, she would do the same for me. No one could have told us that the inevitable cycle of life would assert its dominance, and the tables would turn. Boy, am I glad I was good to my mom.

My mom's passing was bittersweet. I praised God that her suffering was finally over, but I selfishly wanted her here to witness what the Bible calls "the conclusion of the whole matter." In the deepest parts of me I desired for her to see her grandchildren grow up. She had fought so long and hard with me on the cancer battlefield. She was there for the test, and I wanted her to not only jointly receive the passing grade with me, but also celebrate for years to come. Unfortunately, and fortunately, God had other plans.

God and Mom must have been in talks about this book for a while. I knew they were bosom buddies! In the six months prior to her death, Mom asked me a thousand times when I was going to author a book about my experiences. "Write the story, Chantell, write the story. Leave your legacy," she repeatedly pleaded. She never wavered. She never stopped begging me to tell the world about my struggle and overcoming. This book is my mother's dying wish.

MY BREAST LESSONS

⚕ There is no love like a mother's love. Fathers love their children, there is no doubt about that. A mother's love, though, is unique and special. It goes the distance and bears all things. A mother will do whatever it takes. Period.

⚕ Everyone has a cross to bear, but how that giant piece of wood is carried is what counts. My mother carried hers with dignity and grace. She was a model of resilience and fortitude. Her excellent example was invaluable when I was hit with something that was a lot bigger than me, so I thought. Because of my mother, I carried breast cancer like a champ!

⚕ No one can push you toward your purpose like your mama. The world is full of amazing and wonderful people who inspire passion and purpose in others. A mama, however, can do it in a way that no other can. A mother's words are like medicine in a syringe, they go straight to the blood stream. Again, dads are a life force, but even experts agree that the relationship between a child and mother is simply different.

⚕ Taking care of others amid your own suffering is a calling and a gift. Even as my mother suffered with strokes and various other health issues, she consistently showed up for me in my darkest hour. In turn, I will make certain to emulate her in that regard.

My Husband

*"I have a tender place in my heart
when I think about the way he handled me
with such care for the duration
of my battle."*

B efore I tell you about my husband's reaction to my diagnosis, let me provide you with insight concerning his personality. First, he is a good man. It's like when the elders tell young women to "find yourself a nice young man to settle down with, get married, and have some babies." He's that young man. Boy, I'll tell you, I was happy to get a man that loves God and his mama! Although, his mother has passed on, he still honors, loves, and cherishes her as much as he did when she was still among us.

Something else you should know about my husband is that he is a "techie." As the proud, long-time founder and CEO of a network engineering company, he is a superhero of building and maintaining firewalls for computer systems. For those who may not be familiar with computer jargon, a firewall is a security system created to block unauthorized access into a computer network. Surely, cancer would be a serious breach of my body. The most prime example of an unwanted and unwelcome guest.

I'm sure you can imagine what happened when I walked into the house that fateful day after leaving the radiologist's office. Keep in mind also that I dodged his phone calls the entire ride home, so he was posted up when I stepped my tennis shoe through the front door. The moment I encountered him in the hallway after getting my daughter settled in, the façade I held on so tightly in the car fell apart. Though the radiologist had not given me a hard confirmation of a cancer diagnosis, the mere thought of it scared the socks off me. The words "abnormal cells," the damning hug from the nurse, the expressions on the faces of the staff, none of these gave off an "aww, it's probably nothing" vibe. Something didn't feel right about the whole thing, and I was scared.

My husband could feel the unsettling in my spirit when I collapsed into his arms in the hallway. As I related what transpired in the radiology room, my emotions said, "you can pretend if you wanna, we are about to be free." Before I knew it, I was bawling out of control (bawling here refers to crying like a newborn baby, not to be confused with *balling* out of control like football players and rappers do). True to form, my big, strong husband just held me and let me have my moment. When I was done with catharsis, he assured me that everything was going to be alright.

A few weeks later, when the call from my primary care doctor delivered Zeus' thunderbolt containing the news of my breast cancer diagnosis, my husband went right into resolution mode. I will tell you, that man was NOT playing about me! I honestly believe that his relationships with computers changed that day. He is a network engineer. He builds and maintains firewalls for computer systems. Who would have known that he would be a firewall between me and breast cancer. Suddenly and unexpectedly, he enlisted them as an ally to repair and recover me.

One thing that stands out very clearly in my mind is the way my husband indulged my every whim while I was going through chemo treatments. I chuckle to myself sometimes because I'll bet he thought cravings were just for pregnancy. Well, my cancer journey showed us both that this is absolutely false! One day I might sit down with my husband and tabulate the number of Giordano's and other junk food runs he made in the middle of the night. I'm sure it was in the hundreds! Okay, that's a slight exaggeration, but the point is that he was all over the outrageous chemo requests. I should have started a group called Cookies for Chemo. Not a bad idea. I still may do that.

My husband REALLY activated his computer gangster when he used it to secure one of the best cancer surgeons. Time was no match for him when he jumped immediately online to contact the top-notch doctor that had been recommended to us by a trusted source. Now, hear me when I say this. When he reached out to this distinguished medical professional the first time, he was told that there was no way services could be procured swiftly. The doctor was away speaking and was much too busy to tend to the needs of little ole me. Well, suffice it to say that within a few days we not only heard back from the doctor personally, but I was on the books for a consultation. This well-known, highly trained medical professional was a critical piece to my treatment puzzle. Dang, my husband made that thing happen!

I shouldn't be surprised, though. Cancer and my husband had met in a back alley before under confrontive circumstances. His mother died a few years before from two different types of cancer that ravaged her body in synchronicity. My husband and I had only been married a short time when I watched him stand by her like a tree during her struggle. He never said it, but I know it tore him up inside. That is why I have a tender place in my heart when I think about the way he handled me with such care for the duration of my battle. I'm quite sure visions of the death specter danced in his head. He had watched his mother die a slow, agonizing death from the same insidious intruder that had now taken his wife hostage. Déjà vu must have been the DJ playing the cancer song in his head on repeat. Would I meet the same fate as his mother?

Many of these thoughts are speculations. You

see, my husband, like the rest of my family, is an immediate action taker. He typically does not display overt emotionalism. Therefore, any thoughts of doubt, fear, or uncertainty would never have been made audible to me or anyone else. He just attacked the issues head on and focused on the resolution. He was the tech expert on the team and played the heck out of his position. He was solid and always right on time!

MY BREAST LESSONS

🎀 My husband was an excellent example of refusal to take no for an answer. Had he just accepted that the cancer specialist had no availability for me, who knows if things would have turned out as well as they did.

🎀 Observing my husband through my journey taught me that care and concern doesn't have to be loud. He quietly and unassumingly went about the business of making every effort to make me feel as comfortable and secure as possible. Few words, many actions.

🎀 I am still in awe at the strength of this man who watched his mother be eaten alive by the same disease that threatened the life of his wife. He manifested both strength and gentleness with both leading ladies in this life.

Son

"I'm Mommy's heartbeat."

One of the first thoughts that entered my mind when I received that call on that Wednesday in 2017 was, "I have to be okay. Who's gonna cook the chicken and biscuits?" I was feeling indignant. I went through hell getting that little boy here and I planned to be around to raise him. Let me explain.

After several miscarriages, I had trouble conceiving. My husband and I tried everything in the book to make it happen, but it just wasn't working. I think now about those couples on TV who talk about spending thousands of dollars on fertility treatments, just to be bitterly disappointed time and time again. That was us. The anguish and heartbreak we felt every time we took a pregnancy test that came back negative became unbearable. We are a couple of faith, but, geez, was it necessary to test it to that extent?

Then it happened. We got the news we wanted to hear! All the money, tears, missed workdays, and painful shots paid off. It was a moment when I knew God's power was real. The last round of fertility treatments was successful, and we were going to have a bouncing baby boy! Well, we didn't know it was a boy at the time, but we didn't care. We just wanted a healthy child to love and raise to the best of our abilities. Finally, my biggest dream and wish had come to pass.

Therefore, I didn't act as soon as I should have when those abnormal cells were found during a routine exam. I had just had the baby I believed God for, and I was laser focused on taking care of him, my family, and working. Nothing else mattered besides my family and job. If you have ever wanted and hoped for something so badly that it became an obsession, you can relate. In fact, I kept missing mammogram after mammogram appointment because I had gotten complacent. By the way, that was NO excuse. Complacency in this area will kill you! Then to further add insult to my own injury, even after I was told that there were abnormal cells found in my breast tissue, I *still* didn't go back for a follow up. The journey to motherhood was going well, and I didn't want to disrupt that process. To this day, that burns in my soul. I constantly wonder if I could have avoided progression to Stage 2 breast cancer if I had just followed through.

My son's existence gave me the will and strength to fight on a whole different level. I believe they call it indominable will. I had gone through too much, for too long, to have this child and I planned to be here to see this mommy thing through. I will never forget the day he reminded me that he, besides God and my family, was my biggest assignment on this Earth. The day I shared the news with my mom, he was playing in the living room. At what had to be a God-ordained moment, he came up and wrapped himself around my leg. My son was reminding me that giving up wasn't an option.

I count it as a blessing that he doesn't remember much from chemo and radiation days. Daycare took care of him for me while I was going through it, and by the time he was picked up, I was resting. Fortunately, there wasn't much of a need to explain what was going on because he was so young. He just knew that mommy was really tired. Eventually, he smelled something rotten in the state of Denmark when I "disappeared" around the time of the surgery. "Where's Mommy," he kept asking. I'm still not sure what answer he was given, but it must have appeased him, at least for the time being.

When I came home from the hospital after having a double mastectomy, he was beyond excited to see me. You should have seen his little face. "Mommyyyyy!" he squealed, taking off at top speed toward the chair I was sitting in. Family members were on the job, cautioning him not to run into me. He slowed down, walked carefully over to a chair, and pulled it up right next to me. "Mommy, I just want to be close to you," he expressed tenderly. There he sat, quietly smiling, happy his mommy was home.

My son saved my life in so many ways throughout this ordeal. He saved it through breastfeeding when he rubbed on my breast and said, "Mommy, what's that?" Curious, I felt it and realized that something was there. I dismissed it, thinking it was most likely a clogged milk duct. It wasn't until I stopped nursing that I noticed the lump was still there. Truthfully, I did not go to the doctor to get it checked out as soon as I should have. This pattern of behavior kept showing up repeatedly during this journey. It was a costly pattern, a pattern I am pleading with others not to adopt.

He saved my life by giving me a "why" strong enough to endure the knockdown, drag out battle with breast cancer. Anyone who knows me knows how much I adore my family, but there is a special bond between a mother and son. He is my miracle baby, the gift I pleaded with God to shower upon me. He will forever remember that he is mommy's heartbeat because everyone needs a heartbeat to live.

MY BREAST LESSONS

ॐ The innocence and purity of a child can cleanse the spirit and soul. It doesn't always take a whole lot to satisfy them. Sometimes, something as simple as grabbing a chair and sitting in your presence creates a safe space where they feel loved and nurtured.

ॐ During the roughest, toughest life challenge to date, my son was a constant reminder of why I had to keep going. He didn't ask to come here, so it was my duty to fiercely battle anything that tried to take to take me out. His voice, his face, the gentle touch of his little hand are permanent residents in my soul. They never let me forget the "why" attached to everything that I do.

My Siblings

"The battle was given selectively because God knew her strength but the victory was earned and fought individually because she knew her purpose. My first best friend. My warrior. My forever shero. My sister."

My little sister Chrissy is my heart. She's my sister, friend, and daughter all wrapped up as the greatest gift. Though, we are only five years apart, I helped raise her. We are as close as two peas in a pod. If I sneeze in my living room, she says "Bless you" two states over. That's how it is with us. That's how our bond is built. So, you can imagine her reaction when she found out I had Stage 2 breast cancer.

Chrissy was the first person I called after telling my mom about the news. It's scary how alike she and my mother are. I swear they are the same person with different faces. Wait, their faces look alike, too.

Anyway, when I told her what the doctor said, her first words were, "Okay, so what are we gonna do? Are you going to the doctor in the morning? What happens next? What's the plan?" That's my sister. Like our mother, she doesn't do all that emotionalism. She's all about the action.

I have always said that I don't believe my sister knows her own strength. Each time I hear the song "I Didn't Know My Own Strength" by the late, great Whitney Houston I think of her. Throughout our lives we've taken turns carrying each other when we could not individually stand on our own two feet. And stand we did, repeatedly. My mama didn't raise any wimps!

I can recall vividly going from my normal weight of 165 down to 108 pounds. I *had* to look like Skeletor from the He-Man cartoons. Shoot, I think I walked past the floor mirror one time and scared myself! Even with the significant weight loss, vomiting, losing my hair, and chemo treatments, not once did I see my sister cry. I cried the ugly cry, but she didn't. Every word out of her mouth focused on solutions and problem solving. Her positive energy fueled me when I had less than nothing in the tank. I can hear her right now saying, "Okay, next. What do we need to do now?" Oh, I need to add here that she is a single parent of three. Can you say, "superhero status?"

Yeah, my little sister does not play about me. When she wasn't on the phone, she was burning up the road. She used all her vacation time on me in 2017, and we did not go to the Bahamas. Instead, that time was selflessly utilized to hit up social media and call out the village. That horn could be heard around the world! Posts, inboxes, videos, you name it, she contacted every person that our family knew. When the troops were rallied, she gave them marching orders. Meals, house cleaning, babysitting, and errands were all on the list. My sister earned her degree in Project Management during this experience. I only hope that she knows how much I love, respect, and appreciate her. I pray that somehow, someway, I will be able to show her how much she means to me.

Then there's my Mantez, my only other sibling on my mom's side. Since my mom gave birth to him in her later years, but still had to work, he became my baby. He is a gentle giant, but a man's man for sure. When we talk about carrying people in their most vulnerable space, Mantez did that for my mom. Like, he physically lifted her up and supported her weight when she could not take a single step unassisted. He was my mother's caretaker until the very end, and for that, I will be ever grateful.

My younger brother is a man of few words. He lets his actions reveal his truest, realest thoughts. That's why you must watch him closely if you want to know what's going on with him. Otherwise, you'll miss it. Mantez has always done what was needed without comment or question. His stoicism has been mistaken for standoffishness on many occasions, but that's only because those folks don't know him. He despises hospitals the way Superman hates Kryptonite, but there he was every time. My baby brother was right at my side for chemo treatments whenever he could be, despite his feelings about the environment. That same selflessness found in myself, my sister, and my mother shows up in him every day of the week.

This section would not be complete if I neglected to mention my siblings on my father's side. While we do not have as close of a relationship as my mother's children, I still appreciate their existence. Thank you for all that you have done and will do in the future. I am grateful.

MY BREAST LESSONS

🎀 My siblings are my best friends. I don't know what I did to deserve these amazing humans, but I am beyond blessed to have them.

🎀 There is nothing in this world more important than family. When no one else is there, they will be there willing and waiting.

🎀 My cancer blessing revealed the true nature and foundation of my relationship with my baby sister. If I didn't know it before, it is abundantly clear now that we are inseparable.

Sonya

"Sonya's life was a celebration of all that is good and beautiful about the world."

No story about my breast cancer experience would be complete without mentioning my sweet Sonya. Sonya was my baby sister Chrissy's best friend. She was my other little sis, and I loved her like she was my own flesh and blood. If you saw Chrissy, you saw Sonya. Frick and frack were inseparable. She took the sun with her wherever she went, brightening everybody's day that crossed her path. She was one of *those* people, the ones that leave an indelible mark on you forever. Growing up she was that kid that was always at our house. Our wonderful young queen Sonya was an honorary sibling in our household.

Sonya was a real standout young lady. She had the kind of personality that lit up a room without you having to flip on a light switch. She was sweet and bubbly, like a 7-11 Big Gulp drink. You couldn't help but smile when she was around. She loved life and life loved her. It pains me in my soul that I am referring to her in the past tense. I will tell you more about that in just a second.

When I was diagnosed, Sonya was right there in the mix of people waiting and willing to help. Chrissy was my support, and Sonya was Chrissy's support. She never showed worry or sadness while I was battling my illness. Oh, and she was beast with the information! She jumped right on in with the best nutritional information I could ask for. She flooded my Facebook Messenger with the latest findings in cancer research, specifically which foods and vitamins could help the body repair itself. Some days I would catch myself laughing under my breath when I got the notification that I received a message. If I were a betting woman, I would have placed a wager every time one would be from her. Sonya reminded me constantly that I had to eat right to stay tight.

I fondly recall one trip back home to Iowa when some lovely ladies and I piled into my car to travel to my mother's house after a cancer awareness walk. When I looked out amongst the faces to find my people, I immediately noticed Sonya wasn't there. Of course, my first thought was, "What in the world?" Sonya's presence at *any* function related to my illness was guaranteed like a student loan. Chrissy asked if we could make a pit stop because she forgot something. Turned out that pit stop was a surprise party in my honor to celebrate my cancer journey. I couldn't believe it! I knew right away Sonya was in on the shenanigans. Of course, she was. That was her. She was always there, always helping. She even made the amazing banner for my surprise party. It was phenomenal!

Then one day I got the call. Our audacious, gorgeous, incredible ray of sunshine left us far too soon. I can still taste the saltiness of the tears that fell between my lips the day I got the phone call. Devastated and heartbroken are nowhere descriptive enough to convey the feelings that consumed me that day. No one is ever ready for news like that. She was so beautiful inside and out, with a personality that could fill an arena. She was helpful, kind, and selfless. Her mind was always configuring ways to be of service to someone else. Her first thought in any given situation was, "Is everyone alright?" I just didn't understand. I did not want to understand. I only wanted to know why.

Well, I am still awaiting the answer to that question. I had *just* spoken with her the night before she left us. We planned to hang out when I got into town. She had a huge gratitude hug coming for all the positive vibes she consistently sent my way after she found out cancer had come by to rest its feet for a while. Thinking back on it, I'm still perplexed. She asked me to stop and grab her favorite jerk snacks before I hit the road for my visit. To this day, I repeat the narrative that I do not understand. "All things in God's timing," is what I told myself.

Sonya was one of a multitude of women whose

radiance and blindingly magnificent smile hid her inner turmoil. I know I shared this earlier, but I feel that it is worth mentioning again. I often wonder if she knew how valuable and worthy, she was, or if she was aware at one point but life made her forget. Life has a way of doing that. The irony is that she was going to start a women's non-profit organization with a focus on mental health and wellness. That was Sonya, planning to build an entire platform for women to address this topic of epic proportions. She was so adamant about making sure no one felt alone. It deeply saddens me that she never had the opportunity to leave behind her legacy. So I'm going to continue her work.

MY BREAST LESSONS

☘ Sonya's life was a celebration of all that is good and beautiful about the world. Her selfless acts of kindness toward myself and my family will forever remain in my mental Rolodex. Right up until the moment that she left us, she was still helping, still encouraging, and still putting a smile on everyone's face. That kind of light is what the world needs!

☘ The supporter needs support. Sonya was my sister Chrissy's support, who, in turn, was one of my biggest means of upliftment during my battle. It was a beautiful chain of women, arms linked moving in perfect synchronicity toward a common goal. Each one needs one.

My School

"My Burnham family had my back every step of the way."

If I haven't mentioned it before, I am a teacher. This automatically gives me superhero status in some corner of the world, though I'm not exactly sure of which one. Anyone with access to a television or social media over the past two years has been exposed to what it means to be a teacher in this country. Teaching is a distinct type of career. There are so many wonderful rewards if you are in it for the outcome and not the income. I love what I do!

When my colleague and soul sister, Lynda, and I went to my administration and shared the initial test results indicating that there *might* be cancer cells lurking in my body, they weren't too worried. They were accommodating and patient as I repeatedly missed workdays to run back and forth to the doctor's office. The shock came the day I shared the results of my biopsy. I went into my principal's office where my AP (assistant principal) happened to be sitting and dropped the news on them. "Well, it looks like it's cancer, Stage 2 breast cancer." For the first time in the decade that I collaborated with these ladies I saw them cry. They cried with and for me, hugging me with silent reassurance. "Let us know what you need. Don't hesitate to ask."

It's funny how we don't always realize how people view us until something happens. I can testify now that when either victory or tragedy strike, folks' perception of you cannot be masked. The outpouring of love and support from the staff and students at my school was humbling and spectacular! I can vividly recall choking back tears as my colleagues' eyes filled with water after hearing that my diagnosis was definite. "What? It's not fair," one of them protested. "No," I thought, "it's not, but it is what it is," was my immediate thought. I didn't dwell there too long, though, because there was no point. Negativity was not going to give me strength for the fight that lay ahead. Love was going to do that.

I felt love by the boatloads in the days and months that followed my sharing the news. I can clearly recall the day I told my 4th graders that I had cancer. I could tell that most of them didn't know exactly what it was but had heard of it and figured out that it wasn't good. A co-worker and I held a question-and-answer meeting in my classroom, which went over surprisingly well. Remember that show "Children Say the Darndest Things?" Well, they did that day, but the discussion proved them to be mature and inquisitive.

My family at Burnham School will never fully understand how they filled my bucket beyond overflow with their show of love and support. There were standout moments that will be permanently tattooed in my memory. I can still feel the endorphins released in my brain when I think about the wonderful surprise I got from our school basketball team. I was asked to attend a basketball game one afternoon shortly after I shared my diagnosis with the students and staff. When I got there, those sneaky rascals had on t-shirts saying "Burnham vs. Breast Cancer" in support of me! Everyone was wearing the shirts, including my fantastic colleagues. Talk about a high moment! It made me feel like ten million bucks! Shortly afterwards I learned that Mr. Lee and Ms. Shazer were the masterminds behind the shirt designs. I wonder if they really know how special they made me feel.

Now, anyone who has known me for more than 24 hours will find out about the love affair I have with the Chicago Bears. See, now get your mind out of the gutter. Not *that* kind of love affair. I meant my love for the game of football. I have been a football fan for as long as I can remember. The word fanatic might be a more accurate adjective. Knowing this, can you imagine how ecstatic I was when I looked up and Sam Acho of the Chicago Bears was standing in my face? Wait, what? One of the Chicago Bears was at *my* school to see ME? You have no idea what that meant to my heart and my healing. On top of that, an invitation to a

Bears game was on the table. I'll bet cancer didn't know it would kick off all these blessings!

As they say in those late night informercials where they sell fancy knives that can allegedly cut through concrete, "Wait, there's more!" My Burnham family had my back every step of the way. My administrators were understanding and supportive when I had to take off work repeatedly for doctor's appointments and treatments. My fellow teachers and staff unceasingly asked how they could help and undergird me, both in the classroom and out. Two dear co-worker friends, who happened to have a close family member with breast cancer, was there for me every step of the way. Students were kind when I showed up at school to teach with a balding head and in excruciating pain. Burnham School created a loving, safe space for me during an exceptionally trying time in my life. Shout out to Burnham School!

MY BREAST LESSONS

🎗 It is a blessing to work in a family environment. Burnham School is more than a place of employment; it is a home away from home.

🎗 Children sometimes understand and process more than we expect. My students were informed and asked intelligent questions about my breast cancer diagnosis.

🎗 You never know where your help is going to come from. I was overwhelmed with the outpouring of encouragement and love from my Burnham family. Words are not sufficient to express my deep gratitude.

Aunt Dee

"Okay, what do we need to do."

A unt Dee, Aunt Dee, classy and sassy, fine as wine. She walks in glamour, and you would be hard pressed to find a hair out of place. This fabulous lady from Iowa is, and always has been, one of my biggest cheerleaders. Aunt Dee is my mother's baby sister, and we are only fourteen years apart in age. Growing up Aunt Dee was a blast! Due to the narrow age difference, we grew up more like sisters than aunt and niece. Make no mistake, though, and please don't get it twisted. It was always abundantly clear who the aunt was, and who was the niece. My auntie did not have to remind me to stay in a child's place. I did that quite willingly on my own.

It is in no way my intent to paint my Aunt Dee as a mean, strict woman. I'm just saying that she ran the ball game, and I knew not to overplay my position. Let's just say our interaction was, and is, quite like the one between my students and I in my classroom. There is an exchange of ideas and an atmosphere of free expression; however, everyone involves knows who the adult in the room is. Remember that James Brown song, "Mama Don't Take No Mess?" Well, there is a version that plays in my head that replaces Mama with Aunt Dee. By the way, my mama didn't take no mess, either.

Considering how we rolled early in my life, it is no wonder that Aunt Dee played such an instrumental role in my cancer care and recovery. When you saw Aunt Dee, you saw me. We were ALWAYS together. This really worked out great for me, especially when she bought new clothes and snacks! When she bought a new outfit, I got a new outfit. I stayed looking sharp. Aunt Dee made sure of it. Between my mother keeping my butter whipped (that's urban jargon for one's hair looking nice all the time), and Aunt Dee keeping me fitted up (young people's term for wearing nice, up to date fashions), I was a walking fashion plate.

Even today, Aunt Dee is always put together. If you're going out with her, you should fully expect diamonds, pearls, a feather boa, or something. She is just gorgeous, period. I call her my Vanessa Williams because I'm thoroughly convinced she easily could have been Miss America. Do you know what else she was? There. She was, is, and always will be, there.

You know how people say things like, "Call me anytime. I mean it. Whenever you need me, no matter what time it is, just reach out and I will be there." Then if you reach out to those same folks after the buses stop running, they suddenly didn't see a missed call from you. Not my Aunt Dee. Her word is her bond every day of the week. With her there are no idioms, cliches, verbal gymnastics. If she says she is going to be there, that's a check you should have no fear of bouncing. You can take her promises to the bank and receive full cash compensation.

When my auntie got the news of my cancer diagnosis, her reaction was identical to my sister Chrissy's. Her first words were, "Okay, what do we need to do." That "spring into action" mindset runs thick and deep through our family. We are solution-oriented analysts who want to know two things upon hearing about a problem: 1) What *exactly* is the issue, and 2) what is required to get it fixed. While we have sensitive hearts as big as all outdoors, the outward show of emotionalism is not our usual mode of expression.

Though our clan doesn't often wear our hearts on our sleeve, it does not mean that the oceans of emotions that we internally experience are any less intense than the next person's. My Aunt Dee is a testament of this fact. I know that her heart was turned inside out when she learned that I had breast cancer. There is no way she was not deeply disturbed and afraid for me. She loves me far too much for that to be the case. What I also know is that she would never let me see her fall apart. That is not her style.

My dashing diva auntie was there for me every step of the way of my cancer journey. She held my hand while I was in the boxing ring with nausea fighting with the free hand. She was the Merry Maids, Top Chef, and Kinder Care all at once. She made endless trips to Chicago to lay eyes on me and see for herself how I was doing. As quiet as it's kept, I don't think Aunt Dee believes anyone can take care of me like she can in the absence of my mom, but that's just between you and I. I do need to ask her how she was able to get my son to eat his broccoli.

I love my Aunt Dee to the moon and back. We have shared a million special moments through the years, but there is one moment that represents an ideal that I have learned to be true. When my grandmother, her mother, took her last breath, I was holding my aunt's hand. We sat together and held each other as my grandma transitioned. This same phenomenal woman was there with me when my mother took her last breath. The circle of life won again. Thank you, Aunt Dee, for being an integral, irreplaceable part of my circle.

MY BREAST LESSONS

✞ The love of an aunt is a special gift. It can be like having a second mother. There is nothing like it in all the Earth.

✞ My aunt is the embodiment of beauty, grace, class, and style under pressure. No matter difficult the circumstances, she consistently showed up with her stuff together.

✞ A person who steps in without being asked and does what needs to be done for the good of the order is invaluable. This is exactly what Aunt Dee always did. You never had to ask, she just jumped right on in.

After The Storm

"I am still here."

Breast cancer is a cross that I wouldn't wish my worst enemy to bear. It disrupts your life, and tries to take everything, including your boobies! As a believer, I hold fast to the notion that if God brings me to it, He will bring me through it. He tested me, and I passed! I am alive! I am still here! I am made to bend but not break!

Coming out on the other side of this thing, I know without a shadow of a doubt that my life was preserved for a reason. I keep hearing the legendary Winans gospel group sing, "Millions didn't make it, but I was one of the ones who did." I did make it. My God, I made it! My life is a gift that I must now share with the world. They say there is no testimony without a test, and this test was like the LSAT! It was hard, extremely hard, but God says I passed with flying colors. I understand that now my duty and obligation is to do everything within my power to assist and guide others through their process.

In my blessing I want to clearly acknowledge

that I did not pass this test alone. There were people sharpening my pencils when the lead broke and grabbing me scratch paper to work out the problems. My people were sitting right in the lecture hall, pouring me coffee, brightening the lights, and nudging my arm to keep me awake though the process. Then there were those monitors who circled around the room, watching me, periodically inquiring if I was okay. Ah, and then there the security guards standing at the gate carefully regulating who was coming and going. It took all these wonderful, amazing people to help me walk out of that lecture hall with a passing grade.

This book is dedicated not only to them, but to every person sitting in the University of Life's classrooms right now. I know it may feel like the exam is too hard and you want to walk right up to the teacher and give back the test as soon as you see what's on it. I know you feel as if you have not been adequately prepared for the subject matter. I know you may be considering dropping the class, or even quitting school altogether. I am here to tell you that you are so much more prepared than you think. You are stronger than you give yourself credit for. Go ahead and finish the exam. There is a passing grade waiting on the other side.

It is my hope that some of the "breast" lessons I have shared throughout this book will bless your life as they have mine. I can remember asking cousin Carol, "Why me?" shortly after I received the news. The responsive words, "Why not you?," made me choke initially. I wasn't ready to hear that, but I'm so glad I did. Those three little words gave me an entirely new perspective regarding my journey, and life in general. I chose to view cancer as a celebration of life and all the wonderfulness it has to offer. Moving forward, I will do my best to honor my mother's memory, greeting each day with a thankful heart. With everything inside of me, I will live and be a testament of God's glory and strength.

Resources

No account of my cancer journey would be complete without sending shout outs to these life-changing organizations.

Non-Profit Support Organizations

Bears Care
Chemo Angels
Sisters Network, Inc.
Cleaning for a Reason
Breast Friends

Facebook Support Groups

I Got This!
Pink Sisters in Christ
Pink Ribbon Freebies
Brown Women Pink
Diep Flap
Breast Cancer Sisters
Finding Humor After Breast Cancer
Breast Cancer Straight Talk

Bible Verses

Jeremiah 29:11

For I know the plans I have for you, declares the Lord. Plans to prosper you, and not harm you, plans to give you a hope and a future.

Hebrews 11:1

Now faith is the substance of things hoped for, the evidence of things not seen.

Psalm 56:3

When I am afraid, I will put my trust in you.

2 Timothy 1:7

For God hath not given us the spirit of fear: but of power, and of love, and of a sound mind.

Matthew 17:20

Our faith can move mountains.

About the Author

"I want to live. I give God the glory and final say over my body and soul. I want to live and be a testimony of his power and strength."

-Chantell Windham

Chantell

"Who's gonna cook the chicken and biscuits?"

Born to Juanita Duplanter and Armell Pate, Chantell Windham was born in a small town surrounded by natural beauty in Newton County, Jasper, Arkansas. She is the oldest of 5 sisters and 3 brothers (2 *siblings being deceased*), siblings from both her parents' sides of the family. Windham was also blessed with having a bonus dad, a man she appreciated more than he may have ever known; (he is deceased). And as Windham grew to adulthood, she wanted a family of her own, so she married and now is the proud mother of two.

Windham's journey would lead her from the state of Arkansas to the state of Iowa, where she attended East High School, Simpson College and Drake University, she continued her studies when she moved to Illinois and attended the University of Illinois at Chicago, and the University of Chicago. Her passion for education has gained her a B.A. in Sociology, MPA, and M.ED.

On a personal note, Windham's hobbies include crafting, working out, shopping, reading, and cooking for her family. It wasn't until the manifestation of her mother's words that she finally shared HER-STORY of how she had cancer, *but cancer never had her.* Although the battle with cancer was challenging, breaking the news to her family was even more taxing. Because of Windham's loyalty, reliability, and known for loving with all her heart, she found herself surrounded by family and friends who became her soldiers in war and the reason for the abundant life she has experienced. Chantell Windham is still here!